A Gefilte Fish Out of Water

By Stacey Haber

A Gefilte Fish Out of Water
Written and illustrated by
Stacey Haber

A catalogue record for this book is available from The British Library

Published by Hope & Plum Publishing *www.hopeandplum.com*

ISBN 978-1-9160363-9-0

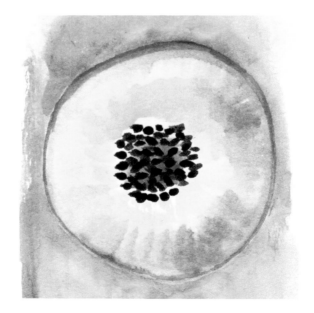

Dedication

To

Moby Mama,
Anna Banana,
Cecil the Sandwich King,
Paula my sister darling dear
Emmackyle

I am who I am because you are who you were.

A Gefilte Fish Out Of Water by Stacey Haber

I've been moving back and forth between London and New York City since 1981. I'm a New Yorker born and bred but my soul is happiest in London. In 1999, with 3 little kids we moved back to the UK for good. But we didn't move to London. After a few years of hideousness in the remote country-sides of Lancashire and West Sussex, the kids and I ended up in a beautiful, commutable village in Hampshire. So remote that we were the only Jews. At least the only evident Jews. It was up to me to make the holidays and prepare the feasts. I found an old, out of print Jewish cookbook in the library and tried to love it, but between us, everything was beige and bland. Nothing like the rich traditions and colourful food of my upbringing. Nothing like the bustling Jewish Kitchen in Whitechapel, near my first law firm at the end of Brick Lane. It became clear that I was going to have to nag friends and family for recipes, rituals and reassurance.

I had an idea of my mother and grandmother's dishes. Julia Child taught me enough technique and muscle memory gave me enough clues to begin. Aunt Ellen's handwritten notebook with additional newspaper cuttings filled in the gaps. I will always equate love with being entrusted tasks in the kitchen as a child and having Aunt Ellen's labor of love cookbook to prepare me for life on my own as a Jewish woman. Passing everything down to my kids gives me the same warmth and feelings of love. Even when we are the only Jews at the table. And we always are.

The lovely cosmopolitan village of Liphook is filled with displaced Londoners and London commuters. What is lacks are Jews. We truly are the only Jews in the village. The only Jews for miles. Our lovely goyishe friends fill the table for each holiday. They read from the Haggadah, recite the prayers with us, and eat our wonderful strange food. We are blessed.

I do have a lovely Jewish friend who is married to a Rabbi in London. I am forever invited to their table and their synagogue, but it's not the same as having my community. I finally found one when my boys were 9 and 10 and I realised they needed to start Hebrew School. I finally found the synagogue by asking a stranger on the street if she knew where it was. It was a safe pick to choose a well-dressed woman early on a Saturday morning. She was headed that way. She took me through the locked gate of a high fence surrounding a small one-story house. The name plate on the gate read *G.& D. J. C.* I suddenly knew anti-Semitism was a thing outside of London.

The food of my new community, the Jewish Kitchen in Whitechapel and my friend in London had the same names as the ones of my childhood, but they were as different as McDonalds and Burger King. Sometimes as different as McDonalds and KFC. I've spent the last 20 years learning new dishes as well as teaching them about my old dishes. I still feel like a gefilte fish out of water sometimes but am strong enough to swim against the stream.

This book is set out according to the holidays of the Jewish calendar. It will help any young person create their own Jewish household and start their owns traditions. Take what pleases you and create new when something doesn't. Let me know when you do though, because I'm still learning myself. Write to me please at stacey@shhh.media.

To life!

A Gefilte Fish Out Of Water by Stacey Haber

ROSH HASHANA

The Jewish new year!

The beginning of hope and helping our chances of being inscribed in the Book of Life for another year. (10 days until Yom Kippur so 10 days to atone and make amends). We start with all things sweet and lovely to signify a sweet year ahead.

On the first night we traditionally dip challah and apples into honey. I've added dipping everything and anything into chocolate.

On the first day, we walk to flowing water and cast away our sins. We use salted breadcrumbs to symbolise life and tears. The fish don't mind. (One year I was too far from any body of water so I flushed them down the toilet. Flowing is flowing.) Next the blowing of the shofar. A seriously difficult instrument to master with a serious sound to make. After the seriousness we feast again. In New York we eat apples, in Israel they eat pomegranates. In Cuba they put hide walnuts. Mi hermano Tio Louie brings the walnuts. Although Cuban and Argentinian, he's with us for all holidays when we're in the same country.

Other traditions are round challahs for a perfect year ahead, spinach to symbolise a green year with plenty of produce, rice for abundance and sweet cakes to portend a year of laughter and joy.

First two Kiddush Prayers

WINE
Hebrew:

בָּרוּךְ אַתָּה יְיָ אֱלֹהֵינוּ מֶלֶךְ הָעוֹלָם
בּוֹרֵא פְּרִי הַגָּפֶן (אָמֵן)

Phonetic:
Barukh atah Adonai, Eloheinu, melekh ha'olam
borei p'ri hagafen

English:
Blessed are you, Lord, our God, sovereign of the universe
Who creates the fruit of the vine

THANK YOU FO R OUR LIVES
Hebrew:

בָּרוּךְ אַתָּה יְיָ אֱלֹהֵינוּ מֶל
שֶׁהֶחֱיָנוּ וְקִיְּמָנוּ וְהִגִּיעָנוּ לַזְּמַן הַ

Phonetic:
Barukh atah Adonai, Eloheinu, melekh ha'olam
shehecheyanu v'kiyimanu v'higi'anu laz'man hazeh.
English
Blessed are you, Lord, our God, sovereign of the universe who has kept us alive, sustained us, and enabled us to reach this season

Round Challah

2 cups lukewarm water
3 pkgs. yeast
8 cups flour
1½ cups sugar
1½ tsp salt
2 sticks (½ lb) butter
5 eggs, beaten (reserve one for glaze)

Directions:

Mix water and yeast in a very large bowl.

Add 3 cups flour and 1 cup sugar.

Let **rise** a half hour in a warm place.

Meanwhile, in another bowl, **add** in 5 cups of flour, salt and ½ cup sugar.

Add butter and cut in with a knife until mixture resembles coarse meal.

At the end of the half hour, **add** 4 beaten eggs to the yeast mixture and stir well.

Add the flour and butter mix. If sticky, add up to two more cups of flour.

Knead well on floured board until smooth and elastic.

Put in oiled bowl and **cover** with towel.

Put in warm place and let **rise** 2 hours (or until doubled).

Punch down. **Knead** lightly for a minute or two.

Divide dough into 3 parts. Set two aside.

Divide the remaining one into 3 equal parts. **Braid and coil** or just coil in a spiral.

Repeat for the other two batches of dough.

Place loaves onto oiled pans.

Cover and let **rise** in a warm place as long as possible (3 hours at least).

Brush the top with beaten egg.

Bake at 350 degrees F/175 C for 45 minutes.

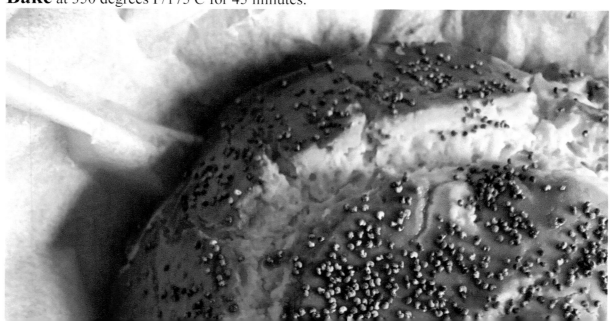

Roast Beast

My family loves a roast beef but in England they love lamb. This recipe works beautifully for both. It also works very well for salmon. My Rabbi Alex and his family are vegetarian, so I also used it for vegetables when they came to me for Thanksgiving once. I mentioned it took me forever to find a synagogue, let alone the right community for us. I knew I had found the right one when during Rosh Hashana services, the rabbi's four year old son, laying on the floor behind the women's section and singing softly to himself, suddenly uttered in a perfect American accent, "Oh man!" The man was drawn out with three a's just the way my kids said it. When his mom laughed along with us, I knew I was home. That was twelve years ago at the time of writing. Alex is still my Rabbi and we have a podcast together now, along with Rev Richard Hayes. It's called *The Rav & the Rev.*

2 lb roast beast
2 tbs chopped rosemary
½ jar of wholegrain mustard
Drizzle of honey or maple syrup
Salt & Pepper

Directions:

Preheat oven to 350 F / 160C.

Spread the mustard all over your beast of choice.

Sprinkle the rosemary, salt and pepper all over as well.

Drizzle the honey or syrup lightly and sparsely.

Cover with foil.

Roast. 2lbs of meat will take 1.5 hours for rare, fish will take 25-35 minutes, veg will likely take an hour depending on size.

Remove foil and roast for another 15 minutes.

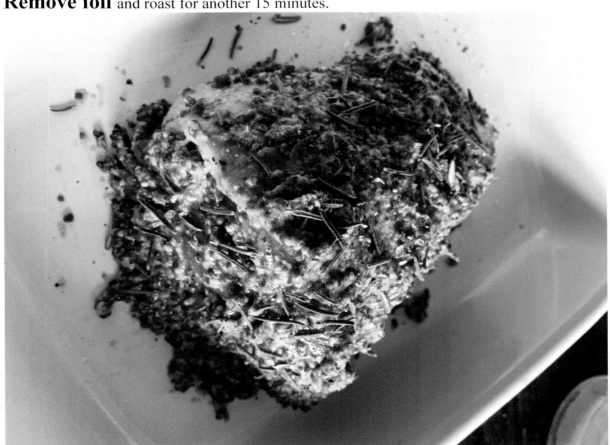

A Gefilte Fish Out Of Water by Stacey Haber

Moby Momma's Stuffed Breast of Veal

Moby Momma was my mother. It was her nickname for as long as I can remember. It's how she signed half her letters to me when I went off to college. She wrote to me twice a week and I've kept the letters. They still make me laugh. When I found them again after a few years after she passed, I thought they'd make me cry. But they didn't! I still laughed. That's how great she was. I'm sure she was the best mother ever in the history of motherhood. MM wasn't a good everyday cook, but she was a **great** Jewish holiday cook. And Italian cook, but that's another book entirely.

This recipe is one of my sister's specialties now. Hers is so good that my kids ask for it every time we visit her in Florida.

1 breast of veal, 4 ribs
1 pot chicken soup or stock, powdered is fine
2 containers chicken fat (my sister likes jarred, I make my own)
1 lb matzo meal, medium coarse
3 large sweet onions, roughly chopped
3 heads garlic, peeled
1 lb baby carrots
½ head celery, inner stalks and leaves
4 eggs
Salt & pepper
Garlic powder
Paprika

Soup:
Into large pot **add** soup, onion, celery and carrots
Bring to a **boil**. Let **simmer** for ½ hour.

Veal:
While soup simmers, **cut** pocket in veal breast lengthwise, without cutting through the sides.

Stuffing:
Drain soup, reserving all vegetables and liquid separately.
Place vegetables, ½ container of chicken fat and garlic into food processor.
Pulse to almost a puree. (If the food processor bowl is full, **remove** to large mixing bowl to add the next set of ingredients.)
Add 2 cups matzo meal and 4 eggs.
If liquid is needed, **ladle** in chicken soup.
Add salt, pepper and paprika (as much as you want but go easy on the salt).
Mix to a thick but moist and sticky consistency.
Add additional matzo meal and soup as needed to expand.

Stuff veal pocket, pressing to make sure the stuffing is all the way thru the from end to end. Overstuff as much as possible. Extra stuffing can be baked along side of the veal either in the same pan on the side or in a casserole. If using a casserole, just make sure to moisten the stuffing after ½ hour with soup.

Ladle enough chicken soup over the veal to coat the bottom of the pan.

Glaze:

To the rest of container of chicken fat, **add** salt, pepper, garlic powder and paprika. Go easy on the salt but add enough of the other spices to make a thick paste.

Brush over entire top and sides of veal.

Roast at 350 F/175 C for 3 hours, basting with additional soup every half hour or so. If the top gets too brown, **cover** with foil. Continue cooking another 2 hours **basting** with pan juices every ½ hour. Make sure the bottom of pan is **never** dry.

Remove from oven after 5 hours and let **rest** for 30 minutes.

This is a low and slow cook. If your oven heats unevenly, keep turning the pan every hour. And keep it moist. I cannot emphasise that enough. Another dish that tastes better the second day. It's a Jewish thing.

A Gefilte Fish Out Of Water by Stacey Haber

Honey Cake

This is the ugliest cake ever. It's a funny khaki mud colour and it's very plain. Traditionally there are no decorations, icing, filling or anything. But everyone LOVES it. Go figure.
I like a wee bit of bling so I dress it up with cream cheese icing. If you need a recipe, email me (Stacey@shhh.media).

1 lb or 1 ¼ cup honey (a whole jar)
1 cup oil (I like corn oil or nut oil but you do you)
2 tsp instant coffee dissolved in ½ cup plus 2 tbs boiling water
½ lb or 1 ¼ cups dark brown sugar
4 eggs
1 lb or 4 cups self-raising flour
1 heaping tsp each cinnamon and mixed spice
1 tsp ginger
1 tsp baking soda

Directions:

Preheat oven to 325 F/165 C.

Mix honey, oil, coffee and sugar.

Add eggs.

Sift then Add remaining ingredients.

Bake in greased dish, approximately 1 hour and 15 minutes.

I love it the next day, toasted with a schmear of cream cheese (yes, even with the icing). It's one of the few cakes that's perfect for tea. I make a big pot and have it all to myself. Well try to anyway.
The English like to stuff it full of dried fruits like currants, cherries and sultanas.
Did you know, the traditional English wedding cake is a fruit cake covered with royal icing?
I had to go all the way back to NYC to get married because I wanted a chocolate wedding cake.

Teigelach

My family eats Teigelach by pulling the balls off with our fingers and popping them into our mouths. I've seen others slice into the pyramid and eat with forks, but that no fun. If you can't eat with your fingers, you're not really partying hard enough.

2 eggs, beaten
2 tbs oil
1 ½ cup flour
½ tsp salt
½ tsp baking powder

Glaze
1 cup honey
½ cup sugar
½ tsp ground ginger
1 cup chopped nuts
½ cup maraschino cherries
Hundreds and thousands, or sprinkles
(I use chocolate chips and mint instead of the traditional sprinkles)

Directions:

Preheat oven to 350 F/175 C.

Mix eggs with oil.

Add flour, salt and baking powder.

Knead.

Roll out to ½ inch thick.

Cut into ½ inch pieces.

Roll into balls.

Bake 12 minutes or until golden brown.

Meanwhile, **heat** honey sugar and ginger, but do not boil.

Add dough balls to hot honey and coat well.

Build into a pyramid.

Sprinkle with chocolate chips, nuts, cherries and hundreds and thousands.

SUKKOT

Jewish Thanksgiving! Celebrating the harvest, it's all about fruit and veg, especially stuffed vegetables. We build a sukkah (booth or hut) outside the home on a patio, balcony, etc. The roof must be made of organic materials and partially open to the sky. It is symbolic of the huts built during the Jews' 40 years wandering in the desert. The Sukkah is used for eating meals, entertaining guests, relaxing and even sleeping. I've even heard it said that it was a mitzvah to have sex in the sukkah. A special place for all my favourite things.

There's a ritual as follows:
Take:

1. the lulav (date palm frond),
2. hadass (bough of a myrtle tree),
3. aravah (willow branch) — these three are bound together and collectively referred to as the lulav, and
4. etrog (a citron, a lemon-like citrus fruit).

They symbolize different types of plants:
-

- good taste and pleasant fragrance (the etrog),
- good taste and no fragrance (the palm),
- pleasant fragrance and no taste (the haddasim), and
- neither taste nor fragrance (the aravah).

By taking all four, we symbolically request that G-d provide sufficient rain for all types of plants and crops to grow and thrive.

They are waved as follows:

- The first three species are held in the right hand, while the etrog is held in the left hand.
- Hold hands apart while saying the special blessing, "Blessed are You, Lord our G-d, King of the Universe, Who has sanctified us with His commandments and commanded us to take the lulav."
- Bring hands together so that the etrog touches the lulav bundle, point and gently shakes three times in each of the four directions – north, south, east and west, then up and down.

Symbolically, this ceremony is a prayer for adequate rainfall for all the vegetation of the earth in the coming year. Our rain dance without much dancing.

A Gefilte Fish Out Of Water by Stacey Haber

בָּרוּךְ אַתָּה יְיָ אֱלֹהֵינוּ מֶלֶךְ הָעוֹלָם
אֲשֶׁר קִדְּשָׁנוּ בְּמִצְוֹתָיו וְצִוָּנוּ
לֵישֵׁב בַּסֻּכָּה (אָמֵן)

English:
Blessed are You, O Lord our G-d, King of the universe, Who has sanctified us by Your commandments, and has commanded us to sit in the sukkah."

Phonetic:
Baruch ata Adonai Eloheynu Melech ha'olam asher kidshanu be'mitzvotav ve'tzivanu ley'shev ba'sukah.

בָּרוּךְ אַתָּה יְיָ אֱלֹהֵינוּ מֶלֶךְ הָעוֹלָם
שֶׁהֶחֱיָנוּ וְקִיְּמָנוּ וְהִגִּיעָנוּ לַזְּמַן הַזֶּה (אָמֵן)

English:
Blessed are You, O Lord our G-d, King of the universe, Who has kept us in life, and has preserved us, and enabled us to reach this season."

Phonetic:
Baruch ata Adonai, Eloheynu Melech ha'olam shehehiyanu ve'kiymanu vehigi'anu la'zman ha'zeh.

When taking the lulav, say:

בָּרוּךְ אַתָּה יְיָ אֱלֹהֵינוּ מֶלֶךְ הָעוֹלָם
אֲשֶׁר קִדְּשָׁנוּ בְּמִצְוֹתָיו וְצִוָּנוּ
עַל נְטִילַת לוּלָב (אָמֵן)

English:
Blessed are You, O Lord our G-d, King of the universe, Who has sanctified us by Your commandments, and has commanded us to take the Lulav."

Phonetic:
Baruch ata Adonai, Eloheynu Melech ha'olam asher kidshanu be'mitzvotav ve'tzivanu al netilat lulav.

Stuffed Cabbage

There's a weirdness about the women in my family line on my mother's side. We all sneeze 5 times every morning. Just the women. The doctors don't know why.

Ironically, making stuffed cabbage has its own weirdness for us. My Grandma Ann made it for every holiday because my mother would always burn it. It would go from uncooked to burnt without warming, no matter how low the heat was. Once Grandma Ann passed, my mother was able to cook it perfectly. Now that my mother has passed, I burn it and my sister cooks it perfectly.

As we live in different countries, I needed to find a way to make it in between our annual Florida trips. My secret is pre-cooked rice, overboiled cabbage and oven baking. The ingredients are the same but mine is more an assembly job before baking. I also add raisins and spray the rice with sushi vinegar because I can't get the sweet and sour tomato sauce here that I could in the States.

Below is the traditional recipe from my grandmother as tweaked by my sister. Email me for baking times rather than top of the stove times, stacey@shhh.media

1 lb ground mince beef
½ cup rice, cooked
2 eggs
3 jars of Hungarian cabbage soup (a secret ingredients not found in my supermarket) or Passata sauce
3 fresh lemons
3 tbs oil
1 head cabbage, parboiled and leaves separated
Salt & Pepper

Directions:
Mix beef, rice, eggs, 4 tbs of tomato sauce, salt & pepper.
Add oil to casserole pot or stock pot with lid or Dutch oven. You get the idea.
Heat the oil over a medium heat until bubbling then reduce heat to a simmer.
Layer the odd or small bits of cabbage over the oil.
Stir.
Spoon 2 tb s meat mixture into a cabbage leaf.
Fold over the hard edge, tuck in the sides then roll up the rest of the way.
Place into the pot.
Continue rolling and layering into the pot with all of the meat mixture.
Heat on low for 30 minutes.
Cover with the tomato sauce and juice of one lemon.
Simmer for another 30 minutes and taste.
Season with salt, pepper and lemon juice as appropriate.

Stuffed Peppers

I know everyone has a stuffed pepper recipe. My mother's had onions and garlic. David's has nutmeg. It's one of the few things I kept from the ex-husband. I also kept his sister, three amazing, incredible children and a penchant for stuffed peppers. Quite a lot to show for 20 years; you'd agree if you met my kids. Before we give him too much praise, let's see if he gets this website up and running as promised…

4 big red peppers
1 bag of **cooked** boil in the bag rice (the fool proof part)
1 jar of salsa
½ lb of chopped meat (I like beef)
1 tsp sugar
1 tsp oregano
¼ tsp nutmeg
Salt and pepper
1 tsp olive oil

Directions:

Preheat oven to 375 F/200 C.

Slice lid off peppers and set aside.

Hollow out insides discarding veins and seeds.

In a bowl, **mix** rice, meat, salsa, sugar, oregano, nutmeg, salt and pepper.

Stuff into the peppers. Over stuff because it will shrink. **Put** lids on peppers.

Place in baking dish.

Drizzle oil over peppers. **Cover** with aluminium foil.

Bake for 40 minutes.

To make this dish vegetarian, add more rice and substitute raisins and nuts for the beef.

A Gefilte Fish Out Of Water by Stacey Haber

Beef Brisket

Brisket is a different cut of meat either side of the pond. In England it is rolled up like a roast beef and roasted. I unroll it and braise it but it seems a shame at over $20 per kg. Sometimes I unroll it, stuff it with herbs, matzoh meal and a beef stock sube crushed and sprinkled, roll it back up again and baked like a roast. Mostly I buy stewing steak and make as per the below. Stewing steak is much cheaper, less fatty and more gelatinous. In the States, I'd stick with brisket. It's all about tradition.

1 tbs vegetable oil
2 lbs beef brisket
2 onions, sliced
2 cloves garlic, sliced
2 parsnips, sliced
1 turnip or small swede, cubed
3 carrots, peeled and sliced
1 tbs paprika
½ tsp thyme
¼ cup nut liqueur
Salt and pepper

Directions:

Heat oil in heavy bottomed pan.

Brown onions. **Add** beef. **Brown**. **Add** garlic, other vegetables and thyme.

Cover with water. **Boil**. **Cover**. **Simmer** for 2-4 hours. The longer the better and more tender. **Remove** meat and veg to serving platter.

Scrape bottom of pan to loosen bits. **Add** liqueur. **Boil** remaining liquid.

Reduce by half. **Add** salt and pepper. **Pour** over beef.

Moroccan Chicken Pie

This recipe is based on one from our lovely posh supermarket, Waitrose. They're so posh, their white label basic products are called Essential rather than Basics. It's the only supermarket that carries Kosher for Passover food in their on-line delivery service. At the entrance to the store there are 9 new recipes per month printed on glossy cards. They're free. I like free.

I've made some changes, because I do that. Spinach and pine nuts are replaced by pecans and mushrooms. I prefer the texture and balance this way. I've also swapped olive oil for butter so it doesn't mix dairy and meat. You be Sinatra and do it your way.

1 tbs olive oil
50g olive oil
4 chicken breasts diced
1 ½ tsp ground cinnamon
50g raisins
50g salted pecans
10 mushrooms, sliced, sautéed in olive oil
200g filo pastry

Directions:

Preheat oven to 360 F/180 C.

Heat baking dish in oven as it's preheating.

In skillet, **brown** chicken in olive oil.

Add cinnamon, raisins, mushrooms and pecans.

Season.

Remove from heat.

Brush baking dish with oil.

Line with all but two sheets of the filo dough. (Brush each sheet with oil after it's in.) Leave some filo hanging over each side of the pan.

Fill pastry case with chicken.

Fold in the overhang.

Cover with remaining two sheets of filo and **brush** whole with oil.

Bake 25 minutes.

For a vegetarian version, substitute hard goat cheese for chicken, and butter for olive oil. I make these individual pies.

A Gefilte Fish Out Of Water by Stacey Haber

Thai Pumpkin Soup

This is a variation on the most popular soup served at the old Number 26 Café in Hampshire, Jane Austen country. Number 26 was a village tea shop and coffee bar founded by a rock n' roll tour chef who wanted to nest and leave the road behind. Imagine chic Seattle coffee bar out front and lacy, chintzy tea room in the back. It worked beautifully and stylishly. That man's a genius; he's back on the road but we have coffee at mine every morning when he's not on tour. And the tea room is now a café across the square. Things change, but this recipe endures.

1 pumpkin or 2 butternut squash
1 tbs vegetable oil
1 onion, chopped
1 inch ginger, peeled and diced
4 tbs Thai red curry paste
450 ml vegetable stock
1 can coconut milk
1 small pot heavy cream
Handful chopped basil
1 tbs sweet chili, optional
Salt & Pepper

Directions:
Preheat oven to 400 F/180 C.
Slice pumpkin in half. **Season** and **roast** for 1 hour.
Scoop out flesh and **mash**.

Heat oil in soup pot.
Add onion and ginger.
After 10 minutes, **add** curry paste.
Add pumpkin, stock, chili paste and coconut milk.
Boil. Lower heat. **Simmer** 5 minutes.

To garnish, **heat** cream and basil together, then **swirl** through soup.

CHANUKAH

The miracle holiday! Festival of lights! It's all about the oil. Here's the story:

They tried to convert us. We said no. They tried to destroy us. We raised an army and fought back. Judah called his army Maccabee meaning hammer. The Maccabees pounded them, reclaimed the temple and relit the Eternal Light. With only enough oil for one night, they sent a rider for more oil. His journey took eight days. Miraculously the lamp stayed lit. We commemorate the miracle by lighting a special menorah called a Chanukkiah. Eight candles symbolises the eight day ride. A ninth candle, the shamush, is used to light the other eight. One on the first night, two on the second and so on. Nowadays we give the kids a gift each night. And we eat fried foods. We are commanded to eat donuts. I love that.

And we let them gamble with the dreidl. A spinning top with letters on each of its four sides: nun, gimel, hey and shin. The letters stand for *nes godol haya shom* which means *a great miracle happened here*. It was traditionally a betting game played for gold coins called *gelt*. Today they are chocolate and covered in gold foil. The rules of the spin are:
-   Nun - nothing happens.
-   Gimel - get all the money in the pot.
-   Hey - get half the pot.
-   Shin - put a coin in the pot.
Good luck!

BLESSING 1

English:
Blessed are You, Lord our G-d, King of the universe, who has sanctified us by His commandments, and has commanded us to kindle the lights of Hanukkah.

Phonetic:
Barukh Atta Adonay Eloheynu Melekh Ha-olam Asher Kiddeshanu Be-mitsvotav Ve-tsivanu Lehadlik Ner Shel khanuka

Hebrew:

בָּרוּךְ אַתָּה אֲדֹנָי אֱלֹהֵינוּ מֶלֶךְ הָעוֹלָם אֲשֶׁר קִדְּשָׁנוּ בְּמִצְוֹתָיו וְצִוָּנוּ לְהַדְלִיק
נֵר חֲנֻכָּה

BLESSING 2

English:
Blessed are you, Lord our G-d, King of the universe, who wrought miracles for our fathers in days of old, at this season.

Phonetic:
Barukh Atta Adonay Eloheynu Melekh Ha-olam She-asa Nissim La-avoteynu Ba-yyamim Ha-hem Ba-zzman Ha-zze

Hebrew:

בָּרוּךְ אַתָּה אֲדֹנָי אֱלֹהֵינוּ מֶלֶךְ הָעוֹלָם שֶׁעָשָׂה נִסִּים לַאֲבוֹתֵינוּ בַּיָּמִים הָהֵם בַּזְּמַן
הַזֶּה

BLESSING 3
This blessing is recited only on the first night or the first time one kindles the Hanukkah lights.

English:
Blessed are You, Lord our G-d, King of the universe, who has kept us alive, and has preserved us, and enabled us to reach this time.

Phonetic:
Barukh Atta Adonay Eloheynu Melekh Ha-olam She-hekheyanu Ve-kiymanu Ve-higgi'anu La-zzman Ha-zze

Hebrew:

בָּרוּךְ אַתָּה אֲדֹנָי אֱלֹהֵינוּ מֶלֶךְ הָעוֹלָם שֶׁהֶחֱיָנוּ וְקִיְּמָנוּ וְהִגִּיעָנוּ לִזְמַן הַזֶּה

England has some of the best donuts in the world now. London has a delicious but overpriced donut in every neighbourhood. The real surprise was Hideout Coffee in Portsmouth. Kickass coffee, smashing donuts and reasonable prices.

I loved my grandparents. All four of them. My maternals were Grandma Ann and Grandpa Morris (who was called Skippy by his friends) and the paternals were Sol and Ceclia. One of the things I loved Grandpa Sol most for was the way he took care of Grandma Celia when she became invalided from arthritis. For the 10 years that I can remember, she was in a wheelchair and he took care of everything, including her. I remember being very young and thinking that someday I would be loved that much too. My father did the same for my mother when she had Alzheimer's for 21 years. Both men are amazing and special to me. Both men are amazing cooks too.

6 potatoes, peeled and grated
3 large eggs
Salt and pepper
Oil for frying

Directions:

Preheat frying pan.

Mix all ingredients.

Shape into patties.

Add oil to pan.

Fry on both sides.

Serve with apple sauce and/or sour cream.

For other proportions, use 1 egg for every 2 potatoes. These are also delicious with sweet potatoes. You can also use a tablespoon of flour to help it bind. I think that makes it claggy. Other people add grated onions, but I don't think the tears are in keeping with such a happy holiday.

I also like strawberry jam when I don't have applesauce in the house.

Fish Cakes

My mother hated fish. Couldn't stand the smell, taste, feel, anything. We couldn't even eat in a restaurant if it had a faint fish odour. She did, however, make the best tuna salad (tuna mayo in England) and salmon croquettes. I never found out why she could cope with tinned fish, especially when she had to de-skin and bone the salmon. Personally, I hate doing that, so I developed a fresh fish recipe. There's something reassuring and secure about knowing that my Mommy could do things I still can't.

1 carrot, grated
½ onion, grated
1 grated radish
2 eggs
½ - 1 cup matzoh meal
½ tsp salt
½ tsp pepper
1 lb fish (salmon and/or any whitefish work best)

Directions:

Mix all ingredients.

Shape into patties.

Shallow fry on both sides in butter or oil over low heat so insides cook well.

N.B. If the mixture still doesn't hold after the addition of the second half cup of meal, add another egg.

Bow Tie Donuts

Traditional yums yums are glazed like Krispy Kreme original glazed donuts in a bow tie shape. They're too sweet for me and I love cinnamon, so I sprinkle and dust. (Not the housework kind. G-d forbid).

1 ¼ cups plain flour
3 tbs confectioners' sugar
2 tbs granulated sugar
½ tsp salt
1 egg
2 egg whites
1 tsp vanilla
Vegetable oil, for frying
More confectioners' sugar
Ground cinnamon

Directions:

Mix flour, 3 tablespoons confectioners' sugar, granulated sugar and salt.

Add whole egg, egg whites and vanilla.

Form dough into ball; **knead** on lightly floured surface 5 minutes.

Cover loosely; let **stand** about 30 minutes.

Heat 2 inches of oil to about 375 F/180 C degrees in heavy, large saucepan.

Roll dough on floured surface.

Cut into 24 rectangular strips.

Twist each strip around twice.

Fry in oil, a few at a time, 3 to 4 minutes or until golden.

Drain on paper towels.

Sprinkle with confectioners' sugar and cinnamon.

Vegetable Tempura

My kids and I love Japanese food, especially sushi. My daughter's favourite fast food place when we lived on NYC's Upper East Side was Teriyaki Boy. Mine was Chirpin' Chicken but I loved TB too. Every so often I make tempura for her so she can have her fix.

In Liphook we used to have a Japanese teppanyaki and sushi restaurant (Benihana meets Yo Sushi) at our local golf course but the Japanese company who owned it sold to an English couple and now it only serves bland food.

1 zucchini
1 carrot
1 sweet potato
1 onion
1 eggplant
1 ½ cups fresh breadcrumbs with chopped herbs
1 tsp salt, loads of black pepper
1 cup club soda or beer
Oil for frying

Directions:

Slice vegetable into oval discs.

Mix breadcrumbs, salt and club soda.

Heat oil.

Dip each vegetable piece into the batter then **drop** lightly into the oil.

Fry until golden on both sides.

Drain onto paper towels.

Sprinkle with more salt.

Make in small batches. Eat one from every batch for quality control.

Fruit Fritters

It's fruit tempura. Not that bizarre really. Always an option in Chinese, Thai and Japanese restaurants. Also McDonalds if you think about it. What else is their apple pie (although it's baked now supposedly) It's amazingly delicious with vanilla ice cream melting on top or a custard puddle underneath. I've been doing the Edinburgh Fringe and dying to try a fried snickers bar. Surely the peanuts count as fruit because they grow on trees.

1 apple, sliced
1 can sliced pineapple, drained
1 banana, sliced
1 mango, sliced
1 cup self-raising flour
½ cup sugar
½ tsp salt
½ cup club soda
Butter for frying

Directions
Mix flour, sugar, salt and soda.
Dip fruit slices in batter and shallow **fry in butter over low heat** until golden both sides.

6

TU BISHVAT

It must be clear by now that Jews love to celebrate. Even the trees have a New Year celebration, and this is it. In the olde days it was about the fruit tithes; today it is about giving to charity and feeding your friends the fruits and vegetables that have been grown in the promised land: sweet potatoes, dates, figs, oranges, almonds, lemons, grapefruits, mangoes, peaches, grapes. The grapes mean more wine in my book.

A Gefilte Fish Out Of Water by Stacey Haber

This recipe comes from Aunt Ellen the cookbook maker. Her daughter, my cousin Jodi has a beautiful glass sculpture collection. Aunt Ellen noticed a small glass sculpture on a credenza in the foyer. It was a lovely glass square with a smaller square of coloured glass in the center. "This is beautiful," Aunt Ellen remarked. "Ma, it's a Glade air freshener!" Sure enough when we looked closer, we noticed the table stood over the dog's basket. Still, beauty is in the eye of the beholder and it was beautiful.

1 large can yams – or two large sweet potatoes boiled and peeled
½ stick butter
2 eggs
Marshmallows
Cinnamon to taste

Directions:
Preheat oven to 300 F.
Grease a deep dish pie pan.
Mash the yams with a little water (or the liquid from the can).
Add the butter and eggs. **Mix**.
Spread evenly in the pan.
Place marshmallows on top.
Bake about 20 minutes until golden.

In England it is nearly impossible to find a bag of white marshmallows. There is a proliferation of pastel colour marshmallows which are utterly useless for this recipe. My best advice is to go online and buy a shed load of white marshmallows or buy a jar of Fluff.

Virtuous Carrot and Raisin Salad

I do know that technically all the ingredients are sweet. But carrots are vegetables and raisins are fruit. However you look at it, eating salad is virtuous. Feel good about it.

1 cup shredded coconut (desiccated in England)
1 ½ cup grated carrots
¼ cup raisins
2 tbs lime juice and half grated rind of the lime
½ tsp freshly grated ginger
Handful of rocket (arugula)

Directions:
Combine, chill and **serve**.

Still don't feel virtuous? Donate some money to charity. Alzheimer's in memory of my mother or MS Society/Alie's Fund For Children With MS for my cousin Alie.

A Gefilte Fish Out Of Water by Stacey Haber

Tzimmes

This is the dish my kids want for every holiday. They love it. Can't blame them as it's the perfect combination of a savoury, meaty, sweet, heart warming, homecoming. A hub in a bowl. Lots of people on both sides of the pond use carrots instead of sweet potatoes but it was always yams growing up. I now use fresh sweet potatoes and only make it when they're in season. A few years ago I couldn't get sweet potatoes in time for Rosh Hashana. Luckily, the times they are a changing. I also can't get flanken or skirt steak here. Specialty butchers do have something called skirt, but it's not skirt steak as we New Yorkers know it. So I use a slow cooked cut of beef; the best I can find on the day as it varies from day to day. If you cook it long enough, it's melt in the mouth yum and you'll never remember it isn't the glorious flanken of your youth.

4 sweet potatoes - cubed
10 prunes, pitted (fresh or canned)
½ cup brown sugar
½ small jar of honey
Splash of port or red wine or marsala wine
Salt & Pepper
Water

Directions:

Layer all the ingredients in a large pot. I layer in this order, sweet potatoes, meat, sugar, salt, pepper, honey, potatoes, meat, you get the idea.

Pour the splash of alcohol over the top. **Fill** with water. **Cover** with lid.

Boil then Simmer 2-3 hours (until meat falls off the bones or falls apart to the touch).

A Gefilte Fish

43

Carrot Pudding

When I visit my family in Florida everyone makes carrot pudding for me. I love it. It's more like carrot bread in the corn bread sense of things. My cousins Jodi and Heidi are both divine bakers and their carrot puddings tastes virtually the same. Here below is Heidi's recipe but I'm guessing if I asked Jodi for her recipe, it would either be identical or very similar. If you ever need a cake or baking for a special occasion, I recommend Bakers Alie (shameless plug for the family!)

1 pound carrots, peeled and cut in ½-inch slices, cooked
3 eggs
3 tablespoons matzo cake meal (fine ground)
1 teaspoon baking powder
1 cup sugar
1 teaspoon vanilla
1/2 cup margarine, melted
1/8 teaspoon cinnamon
Salt and pepper

Topping
2 tablespoons margarine, softened
3 tablespoons firmly packed brown sugar
1 tablespoon matzo meal
Dash of cinnamon

Directions:

Preheat oven to 350°.

Place cooked carrots and eggs in food processor bowl.

Process until smooth.

Add cake meal, baking powder, sugar, vanilla, margarine, cinnamon, salt and pepper.

Mix for a few seconds.

Pour batter into greased 8x8-inch square pan. (You can double the recipe and use a 9x13-inch pan.)

In small mixing bowl, **combine** margarine, brown sugar, matzo meal, and cinnamon with two knives.

Sprinkle topping over carrot batter.

Bake for 45 minutes or until set.

Fig and Orange Salad

The first time I ever had fruit in a green salad was at Babs' house. Babs is Asian and has taught me how to cook Indian. But as much as I love her, this story isn't about Babs. It's about Reyne.

Reyne introduced me to Indian food while we were in law school. I remember the first time more for the walk home than for the food though. We were walking to…can't remember…near Russell Square and she was animatedly telling a story about her father when all of a sudden there was a loud *Boingggggg*. Reyne had walked into a parking meter and it actually made that cartoon sound. She was doubled over from both pain and laughter and it took a full two minutes before she could speak and tell me she was okay.

Reyne was my best friend in law school and my rock or many years after. We worked for the same record company, named my youngest child together and saw the world from the same cracked lenses.

1 bag salad
1 can mandarin orange segments, reserve juice
2 tablespoons lemon juice
¼ cup olive oil
1 tsp oregano
2 tablespoons sugar
1 tsp ground cinnamon
4 figs, sliced (or ¾ cup dried figs, chopped)
¼ cup chopped toasted almonds
Salt and Pepper

Directions:

Mix orange juice, lemon juice, oil, sugar, oregano, cinnamon, salt and pepper.

Mix salad leaves, orange segments, figs and almonds.

Pour dressing over just before serving.

In England fresh oranges and mandarins tend to be tart rather than sweet. If you prefer it tart, substitute fresh for the caned.

As for the bag of salad, I prefer Rocket (arugula in the US), Spinach and Watercress. The peppery leaves of the rocket and watercress counterpoint the sweet oranges beautifully.

Grilled Fruit

I love England. I am my best self here. I also love fruit. Fresh fruit is always plentiful and affordable here. It's just one of the many, many things England does better than the rest of the world. They're even learning to BBQ. The world is teaching them very well. This recipe combines the best of all parts of the world. It's the UN of dessert.

Peaches, halved and stoned
Apricots, halved and stoned
Oranges, sliced thickly
Apples, halved and cored
Fresh figs, halved
Fresh dates
1 tbs butter
1 tbs honey
Salt and pepper
Squeeze of lime juice

Directions:

Melt honey and butter together. Season.

Arrange fruit on a hot BBQ grill.

Brush marinade over.

Cook 2 minutes.

Flip fruit.

Brush again.

Grill 2 minutes.

Squeeze lime over.

Serve with yogurt or ice cream. If you can't catch a dry sunny day for BBQing you can always grill them indoors. There's a joke in England: If you don't like the weather, wait 5 minutes. It will change. I think it's a joke…

In NYC it's the opposite, if you don't like the weather, too bad.

PURIM

This is another 'they tried to annihilate us" holiday where we feast and drink copious amounts of wine. It involves a King, his Queen, her uncle and the King's evil advisor. It happened in Persia. So far it sounds like Aladdin without the genie. Where it digresses is with the attempted genocide and the woman saving the kingdom. In a nutshell, the King married Esther, a Jewess. The King's advisor, Haman, demanded that everyone bow to him to satisfy his ego which was roughly the size of his distended gluttonous belly. Mordecai, being Jewish would not (because Jews don't kneel before false idols). Haman knew this and used it as an excuse to order the murder of all Jews. Esther revealed to the King that she was Jewish. Haman was killed instead.

From this we get:
The reading of The Book Of Esther (the Megillah)
The eating of Hamantaschen
The making of noise - screaming, banging, drumming – whenever Haman's name is mentioned in the reading of the Megillah.

The purpose of the noise is to remind everyone, especially children, that we must retell our stories and never remain silent about those who want to destroy us. Just like they have to tattle on bullies. Indifference to genocide is as great a crime as genocide itself.
Other observances include giving gifts of money to the poor, feasting and sending food to friends.

Before eating bread, recite the following prayer: Hebrew:

בָּרוּךְ אַתָּה יְיָ אֱלֹהֵינוּ מֶלֶךְ הָעוֹלָם הַמּוֹצִיא לֶחֶם מִן הָאָרֶץ.

Phonetic:
Baruch Atah Adonai, Elohaynu melech ha'olam ha-motzi lechem min ha-aretz.

English:
Praised are You, Adonai our God, Sovereign of the Universe, Who brings forth bread from the earth.

Before drinking wine or grape juice, recite the following prayer:
Hebrew:

בָּרוּךְ אַתָּה יְיָ אֱלֹהֵינוּ מֶלֶךְ הָעוֹלָם בּוֹרֵא פְּרִי הַגָּפֶן.

Phonetic:
Baruch Atah Adonai Elohaynu Melech Ha'olam borei p-ri ha-gafen.

English:
Praised are You, Adonai our God, Sovereign of the Universe, Creator of the fruit of the vine.

Before eating foods such as cakes and cookies, recite the following prayer: Hebrew:

בָּרוּךְ אַתָּה יְיָ אֱלֹהֵינוּ מֶלֶךְ הָעוֹלָם בּוֹרֵא מִינֵי מְזוֹנוֹת.

Phonetic:
Baruch Atah Adonai Elohaynu Melech Ha'olam boray meenay mezonote.

English:
Praised are You, Adonai our God, Sovereign of the Universe, Who creates various kinds of food.

Before drinking all other food and drink: Hebrew:

בָּרוּךְ אַתָּה יְיָ אֱלֹהֵינוּ מֶלֶךְ הָעוֹלָם שֶׁהַכֹּל נִהְיָה בִּדְבָרוֹ.

Phonetic:
Baruch Atah Adonai, Elohaynu Melech Ha'olam sheh ha-kol nihyeh bid'varo.

English:
Praised are You, Adonai our God, Sovereign of the Universe, Whose word brings all things into being.

Hamantaschen

My youngest son and I baked hamantaschen every year for his class. The tradition started when he was in Reception (Kindergarten in the US). He brought home a cigar shaped pastry and a strip of paper explaining what they learned in RE (religious education) that day. It purported to be hamantaschen but it wasn't even close. No way was I going to let them teach Judaism so poorly. We baked up a batch of apricot hamantaschen and brought them in the next day with a little rolled bit of paper of our own. It explained that they were tri-cornered because Haman wore a triangle hat and had funny triangle shaped ears; and when we ate them, we destroyed Haman, the bully. The kids loved that.

Dough:
1 cup shortening
1 ½ cups sugar
3 eggs
1 tsp vanilla
3 cups flour
1 tbs baking powder
¼ tsp salt

Filling:
1 jar apricot preserves and/or
1 can prune pie filling and/or
1 jar strawberry jam and/or
1 can blueberry pie filling and/or
1 jar Nutella, etc.

Directions:

Preheat oven to 325 F.

Cream together the shortening and sugar.

Add the eggs and vanilla. **Mix.**

Add dry ingredients. **Mix.**

Roll on floured board.

Cut with a round glass or cookie cutter.

Drop a teaspoon of filling onto center of each round.

Pinch sides together to form triangles.

Bake about 30 minutes until golden.

Poppy seeds are another popular filling on the lower East Side of New York. Not my cup of tea, but you go for it if that appeals.

Wine is a very important element of this holiday so it would be folly to not include a wine recipe. Noise is also a key, so the sauce will make the pan sizzle loudly. It also no secret that Chinese food is the traditional Jewish Sunday lunch in New York. This recipe ticks all those boxes.

½ pound ground turkey or extra lean beef
1 cup cabbage, finely minced
2 green onions -- minced
1 egg
2 tbs soy sauce
40 Wonton skins, cut into 2-inch squares
Vegetable oil for frying
Water for sealing skins
1 cup wine (use whatever you are drinking)
½ tsp rice wine vinegar
Cornstarch for dusting
Salt and pepper

Directions:

Mix turkey, cabbage, onion, egg, 1 tablespoon soy sauce, salt and pepper.

Dust board with cornstarch. Place a wonton on the surface.

Drop a rounded teaspoon of filling in center of a wonton skin.

Moisten the rim of skin with water. **Bring** opposite sides together to form a triangle.

Pinch corners together and pleat edges to seal.

Heat a large frying pan over low heat. **Add** vegetable oil to hot pan. **Increase** heat to medium-high

Fry pot stickers closely together until bottoms are golden brown, about 2 minutes.

Watch carefully to prevent burning.

Add ½ cup water to pan and **cover** immediately. Steam until skins are translucent, about 3 minutes.

Uncover and remove pot stickers. Let water **evaporate**.

Add wine, vinegar and soy sauce to pan and let **reduce** by half.

Serve the reduction as the dipping sauce.

Kreplach

It doesn't get more Jewish than a bowl of kreplach soup. Well maybe chicken soup with Matzo balls, but it's close. And chopped liver, gefilte fish, kippered salmon…ok fine. If you shape the filled dough into triangles you get to destroy Haman in two courses of the meal. That's mighty good.

DOUGH:
1 ¾ cups flour
2-3 eggs
½ tsp salt
3 Tbs oil

FILLING
1 cup ground cooked beef or chicken
1 small onion, grated
1 tsp. salt

Directions:
Boil a very large pot of water or stock (see chicken soup recipe below).

DOUGH:
Combine dough ingredients. Use two eggs only at first. If and only if it doesn't come together after kneading for 5 minutes, add 3rd egg. (Altitude, humidity and egg size will vary)
Knead and **roll** out thin on floured board.
Cut into 3-inch squares or circles.

FILLING:
Mix filling ingredients well.
Drop 1 tsp of filling into center.
Moisten edges with water and **fold** into triangles.
Boil approximately 20 minutes until kreplach float to top.

You can eat them in soup if using stock or you can eat them as a dish like dumplings. Alternatively, you can sauté them:
Heat oil over medium flame in 10-inch skillet. Sauté boiled kreplach until golden brown on both sides.

Tip:
The dough will roll out more easily after being wrapped
in a damp cloth for an hour or refrigerated for 20 minutes.

A Gefilte Fish Out Of Water by Stacey Haber

Hassleback Potatoes

I love potato chips/crisps. I'm a little addicted. Ic an only eat the l=plain salted kind but I don't mind. I love them. As I've been on a diet since birth (even though I only weighed 5 pounds then) I've always had to lose at least 5 pounds, more often 20 pounds. So this is a great recipe for when I'm jonesin' for crisps but don't want to lose the Fatty McFat Fat plot entirely. When I cook them extra long and let them go crispy they satisfy the noise requirement for a Purim dish.

4 large potatoes
2 tsp olive oil
1 sprig rosemary leaves
Salt and pepper

Directions:

Preheat oven to 425 F / 200 C.

Lay two wooden spoons on either side of a potato.

Slice the potato every ¼ inch just down to the spoon handles. Not all the way through.

Slice all 4 potatoes.

Drizzle olive oil over and into the cuts.

Sprinkle salt, pepper and rosemary over them.

Bake for 1 hour.

Luchen Kugel

The crispy bits are my favourite part of this noodle pudding. Not that pudding is an apt translations for my family's recipe. Some families make it sweet with raisins, cinnamon and cottage cheese. I prefer it savoury with just chicken fat or olive oil or butter, and salt and pepper.

My other used a rectangular pyrex dish for her luchen kugel and both the bottom and the top always came out crispy. Even though I use a baking dish that looks the same, my bottom is never crispy. (Maybe I should consult Mary Berry about that one.)

1 bag wide noodles, cooked
1/3 cup chicken fat, butter or olive oil
2 eggs, beaten (optional)
Sat & pepper

Directions
Preheat oven to 425 F / 200C
Mix all of the ingredients.
Place into the baking dish. And distribute out evenly ensuring that there are sticky up bits to crisp.
Best for 30-40 minutes until golden on top.

Occasionally when I'm using olive oil, I add fresh basil and mozzarella. It's no longer luchen kugel but it is delicious. Email with name suggestions for this variation please. Something Jewish and Italian. stacey@shhh.media.

PASSOVER

Also known as the:
- *Let Me People Go* holiday
- *Prince of Egypt* holiday
- *Ten Commandments* holiday
- Exodus holiday
- Pilgrim holiday

It's a great story told many times. And that's the main point of Passover, the retelling of the Exodus from Egypt and what my Father did for me so we could be here today (but next year in the land of Israel, except in my family where it's next year in the Bahamas).

It's an epic tale that has everything. A hero named Moses. A villain named Pharoh. He's so evil he only gets a title and his real name is never mentioned. I'm pretty sure it wasn't Tom Riddle. It has daring escapes, swarms of plagues and the saving of children. It has a happy ending as well. For those realists who don't like skipping the tragedy it also has slavery, bugs, mass murder and 40 years of wandering in the desert. I prefer to cook on the bright side of life though.

The book we read from is called the Haggadah. There are as many versions as there are types of people. My family have always used the free one from Maxwell House coffee. Let me know where to get free ones in England please. I'd love to see them.

The important elements are: keeping Kosher For Passover (matzoh!), wine, the four questions and the retelling of the tale, especially the 10 plagues. The name Passover come from the 10th plague. On the night G-d smote the first born sons of Egypt, he passed over the houses that had smeared lambs blood on the door frame, namely the Jewish houses. G-d gave Moses the secret signal and Moses gave it to his people. There's so much more to say which is kind of the point. Come for Seder and get the whole story. I'd love to have you.

A Gefilte Fish Out Of Water by Stacey Haber

Hebrew:

מַה נִּשְׁתַּנָּה הַלַּיְלָה הַזֶּה מִכָּל הַלֵּילוֹת?

Phonetic:
Mah nishtanah ha-lahylah ha-zeh mi-kol ha-layloht, mi-kol ha-layloht?

English:
Why is this night different from all other nights?

First Question

Hebrew:

1) שֶׁבְּכָל הַלֵּילוֹת אָנוּ אוֹכְלִין
חָמֵץ וּמַצָּה. הַלַּיְלָה הַזֶּה בְּלוֹ מַצָּה?

Phonetic:
She-b'khol ha-layloht anu okhlin chameytz u-matzah, chameytz u-matzah. Ha-lahylah ha-zeh, ha-lahylah ha-zeh, kooloh matzah?

English:
Why is it that on all other nights during the year we eat either bread or matzoh, but on this night we eat only matzoh?

Second Question

Hebrew:

2) שֶׁבְּכָל הַלֵּילוֹת אָנוּ אוֹכְלִין
שְׁאָר יְרָקוֹת הַלַּיְלָה הַזֶּה מָרוֹר?

Phonetic:
She-b'khol ha-layloht anu okhlin sh'ar y'rakot, sh'ar y'rakot. Ha-lahylah ha-zeh, ha-lahylah ha-zeh, maror?

English:
Why is it that on all other nights we eat all kinds of herbs, but on this night we eat only bitter herbs?

Third Question

Hebrew:

(3 שֶׁבְּכָל הַלֵּילוֹת אֵין אָנוּ
מַטְבִּילִין אֲפִילוּ פַּעַם אֶחָת.
הַלַּיְלָה הַזֶּה שְׁתֵּי פְעָמִים?

Phonetic:
She-b'khol ha-layloht ayn anu mat'bilin afilu pa'am echat, afilu pa'am echat. Ha-lahylah ha-zeh, ha-lahylah ha-zeh, sh'tay p'amim?

English
Why is it that on all other nights we do not dip our herbs even once, but on this night we dip them twice?

Fourth Question

Hebrew:

(4 שֶׁבְּכָל הַלֵּילוֹת אָנוּ אוֹכְלִין
בֵּין יוֹשְׁבִין וּבֵין מְסֻבִּין.
הַלַּיְלָה הַזֶּה כֻּלָּנוּ מְסֻבִּין?

Phonetic:
She-b'khol ha-layloht anu okhlin bayn yosh'bin u'vayn m'soobin, bayn yosh'bin u'vayn m'soobin. Ha-lahylah ha-zeh, ha-lahylah ha-zeh, koolanu m'soobin?

English:
Why is it that on all other nights we eat either sitting or reclining, but on this night we eat in a reclining position?

<u>Cottage Kugel</u>

Two days into Pesach and my children are *so over* matzoh. This dish is a great way to hide it. In America buy small curd cottage cheese. I've never seen it in Britain, but it doesn't really matter.

5 eggs
1 cup milk
1 lb cottage cheese (large tub)
1 tsp salt
½ cup caster sugar
½ tsp cinnamon
2 matzoh, spread with margarine
½ cup ground almonds

Directions:

Preheat oven to 180 C.

Spread margarine on the second side of one sheet of matzoh.

Lay it in a baking dish. You can break it if necessary and overlap.

Whizz the eggs and milk. **Add** the cottage cheese, sugar, salt and cinnamon. **Whizz** again until smooth. **Pour** half over the matzoh in the dish.

Add another layer of matzoh over the cheese mix.

Pour in the rest of the cheese mix.

Sprinkle ground almonds on top.

Bake for 30-40 minutes until top is golden.

A handy tip is to let the cottage cheese drain through a sieve for 10 minutes before using otherwise it can be watery and ugly.

Matzoh Brei

It's matzoh French toast. Just without the toast. Sounds weird but surprisingly delicious.

1 piece matzoh per person
1 egg, per person
1 tsp brown sugar, per person
Pinch cinnamon, per person
Butter for frying

Directions:

Break the matzoh into small pieces.

Mix all ingredients. Let sit for 2 minutes.

Fry in butter like an omelette. Both sides.

Matzoh Pancakes

2 ½ cups milk
1 1/3 cups matzoh meal
4 large eggs
¼ cup vegetable oil plus extra for frying
½ teaspoon salt

Whizz together all ingredients.

Fry like pancakes.
Serve with jam or marmalade.

Passover Blintzes

Blintzes were such a decadence when I was a kid. They come frozen in the US but not that I've ever found in the UK. I will always equate blintzes with my mom and with love because they were always a treat. Potato blintzes with sour cream as a snack when we came home from school or cheese and apple blintzes (one of each) as a special breakfast on the weekend when there was time to cook in the morning. I'm actually welling up as I write this. What I wouldn't give for my mom and her blintzes right now.

Pancakes
3 eggs
6 tablespoons ground almonds
½ tsp salt
Butter for frying

Filling
1 small log of goat cheese, diced or crumbled
1 small apple, diced
1 egg, beaten
Salt, pepper, cinnamon, rosemary

Directions:
Pancakes

Whizz together pancake ingredients. Let **stand** 5 minutes.

Heat frying pan on medium high heat.

Brush with butter.

Pour in enough batter to coat bottom, **swirling** pan to coat evenly. Like making crepes but thicker.

When set and golden, **flip** and cook the other side.

Remove to plate to keep warm.

Repeat until batter all used. My pan size makes 3 pancakes.

Blintzes

Mix all filling ingredients.

Roll filling into the pancakes. (Place filling on bottom end, fold up bottom, fold in sides, roll to top.)

Either **bake** if eating right away **or** store in airtight container in fridge and shallow **fry** when ready to eat.

Serve with sour cream or applesauce for savoury. Or both

When I was testing the recipe I was WhatsApping with Aileen. She suggested having it with ice cream. She's a genius. It was soooo good.

A Gefilte Fish Out Of Water by Stacey Haber

Chocolate Chip Macaroons

I have to order my Passover food online as the nearest Jewish Quarter is too far away. I from Ocado which uses Waitrose products. As posh and expensive Waitrose is, they hardly ever have kosher for Passover macaroons. I have to make my own. Turns out mine are good. The recipe calls for meringue-ing the egg whites, but it works very well with lightly whisked egg whites too. I usually beat the egg whites till I get bored then use them in whatever state they're in. It's all good.

3 egg whites
½ cup powdered sugar
1 tsp vanilla
1 bag (6oz) dark chocolate chips
1 cup shredded coconut

Directions:

Beat egg whites until almost stiff.

Add sugar and vanilla.

Beat until stiff.

Fold in chips and coconut.

Drop onto non-stick cookie sheet or foil lined sheet.

Bake for 15-20 minutes at 350 F/160 C. Do not preheat oven.

Watch 'em carefully, they burn without warning.

As an alternative, melt the chocolate and dip the cooled macaroons for chocolate covered. Also nice is the addition of ground almonds or ground hazelnuts. A cup of either is about right.

Chocolate Torte

This torte is decadent. And delicious. It's even gluten free. Don't be surprised that it doesn't rise. It is Pesach after all.

110 g margarine
225g dark chocolate, chopped
5 eggs, separated
150g caster sugar
140g ground almonds or hazelnuts

Directions:

Preheat oven to 375 F /180 C.

Grease baking dish.

Melt margarine and chocolate slowly. Set aside to cool.

Beat egg whites until stiff.

Cream egg yolks and sugar in separate bowl.

Mix egg yolks and chocolate.

Add ground nuts.

Fold in egg whites.

Bake 45 minutes.

LAG B'OMER

Lag B'Omer commemorates the end of the plague that killed Rabbi Akiva's students (not the Black Plague or Covid-19). It's celebrated with merrymaking: bonfires, barbeques, picnics, dancing and singing. And wine. Of course wine. In ancient times, bonfires were used as signals and warnings. Today they're for roasting marshmallows and singing around (and by today I mean when we are finally free of the coronavirus and can congregate again). I miss live music, especially, Swimmingly, Joe Not Joseph and GoodKid, my favourite bands in 2020. I also miss theatre. The West End, Edinburgh Fringe. Favourite play of the year was *The Man From Verona*.

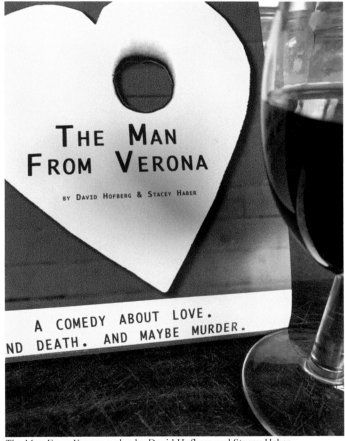

The Man From Verona a play by David Hofberg and Stacey Haber

Satay Burgers

I love satay anything by anyone. Thai satay, Chinese satay, Belgian satay sauce on French fries. I also love hamburgers. This is one of my favourite recipes that I make all year. I have a great Chili Peanut Butter from Applegarth Farm Shop that also works well with this mix when I want a kick. Sometimes I add Frank's Hot Sauce instead. I'm a little addicted to Frank's.

1 lb ground beef
1 jar tahini paste
1 tbs smooth peanut butter.
1 bunch fresh coriander, chopped
Salt & pepper

Directions:

Combine all ingredients.

Form into hamburger patties.

Place on a hot BBQ grill.

Cook until color comes halfway up the burger's side.

Flip.

Grill until required doneness.

Spinach and Lentils

My best friend in NYC, Aileen, is a vegetarian. She sends me NYTimes crossword puzzles and I send her face masks. We've been doing it for the past 20 years. It began with the mail as an easy way to stay in touch but has continued even with WhatsApp, email and FaceTime. Aileen say, "Who doesn't love getting something nice in the mail?" She's right! This is for her. I love this dish and I love her.

1 small package lentils, cooked (reserve cooking water)
1 onion, sliced thinly
¼ cup olive oil
3 cloves garlic, finely chopped
¼ cup chopped fresh coriander
1 bag spinach leaves, chopped (if you have to wash them, squeeze out the excess water)
2 potatoes, peeled and diced, sweet or yellow, your choic
Salt and pepper
¼ cup lemon juice

Directions:

Sauté onion in oil in a large pot.

Add garlic and coriander.

Add spinach.

Stir often for 5 – 6 minutes.

Add potatoes, lentils, and enough lentil cooking water to cover.

Season.

Bring to a **boil**, lower heat, and **simmer** 20 minutes.

Add lemon juice.

N.B. It is even better served cold or room temperature.

SHz

A Gefilte Fish Out of Water by Stacey Haber.

Jewish Penicillin
Aka Chicken Soup

I make chicken soup all the time because I love it and can never, ever, throw away the bones. I even take the bones home from Nando's. Piri-Piri chicken soup is awesome. When the kids were young it was cheaper to get a Family Meal form Nando's than to eat at Burger King. I should have realised then how topsy turvy the world was getting. I'm placing the recipe here because we need some comfort and healing so we can get back to BBQ's and picnics.

My neighbours and I have placed chairs in our tiny front lawns so we can sit outside with a cup of tea, chat and still be 8 feet away from each other. Might have chicken soup in my tea cup.

I never season my chicken the same way twice in a row so my soup is always a new flavour. You choose what you like and roast your chicken that way. If you like garlic and onions, use them, if you're a rosemary, salt & pepper person, go for it. I've had it with pesto, marmalade, hot sauce, sweet chili, lemons & capers, oregano & olives, tarragon, you name it. Always works and always delicious. If you don't season your chicken for roasting, add the flavourings you like into the broth.

Soup
1 whole chicken
6 carrots, 3 for stock and 3 for soup, peeled and sliced
2 stalks celery, both for stock, sliced
Water
Salt & Pepper

Matzoh Balls
Fat from the roast chicken
1 cup coarse matzoh meal
1-2 eggs
Ladle(s) of chicken soup

Directions:
Roast chicken
Preheat oven to 375 F / 200 C
Season the chicken however you like.
Roast until juices run clear and there's no pink in the meat, especially at the joints. I usually give it 45 minute to an hour for a small chicken and an hour to an hour and a half for a large chicken. Keep an eye on it as not all ovens are the same.
Keep the carcass, the fat and the juices straight from the oven. This can be refrigerated or frozen, or used straight away.

Stock
Add carcass, roasting juices, 3 carrots and celery to a stock pot.
Cover with water.
Add salt & pepper.
Bring to a boil.
Cover and simmer for an hour.

Taste. If it's weak simmer for another 30 minutes without the lid. Taste again. Keep going until the stock reduces by about half. Do not let it run dry; you will ruin your pot and stink up your house. You can add a stock cube if you're in a hurry and can't wait for the reduction. Even professional chefs use it; they call it chicken starter.

Remove bones and veg until you have just the clear stock. If you've used a stock cube it will be cloudy rather than clear. That's great too.

Matzoh balls
Mix 1 egg with the chicken fat.
Add the matzoh meal salt & pepper. Mix.
If it's too thick and dry add another beaten egg. It should be like cookie dough.
Ladle in chicken stock until it's moist but not pourable. This will make firm matzoh balls. If you like them soft, add another ladle of stock.
Let rest in fridge for 5 minutes or longer. There's no upper time limit. You can make ahead and refrigerate for two days or you can freeze.

Soup
Add the other 3 sliced carrots to the stock.
Cook over a medium heat for 10 minutes. If shouldn't boil but it's more than a simmer.
Roll out the matzoh balls and drop into the stock.
Bring heat to the boil. When the matzoh balls float, set timer.
Boil for 10 more minutes if you made small balls, 20 more minutes if you made large ones.
Taste and season again.

I serve 5 small, 3 medium or one large matzoh ball per bowl. Different moods demand different sizes. ☺

SHAVUOT

Shavuot the day the Torah was given to the Jews at Mount Sinai. Not to be confused with the giving of the ten commandments (or 15 if you're a Mel Brooks fan). On Passover, the Jewish people were freed from their enslavement to Pharaoh (so they could get an education and work 100 hours a week becoming enslaved to something else); on Shavuot they accepted the Torah and became a nation committed to serving G-d.

It also coincides with the conclusion of the grain harvest which begins at Passover and ends at Shavuot with the wheat harvest. (Not to be confused with the celebration of the fruit harvest which is Sukkot.) Therefor, two loaves of bread are symbolic; hence the saying "two loaves are better than one." I made six loaves. Overachiever.

It is celebrated by customs rather than commandments. The Book of Ruth is read, and dairy is eaten, mostly cheesecake in my family. Greenery and flowers are used as adornments of the home and the synagogue. A fabulous time for extreme grilled cheese sandwiches, goats cheese tarts, more blintzes with sour cream and at least four types of cheesecake.

Rice Pudding

This is comfort food. Way more popular in England than in the States. Don't ask me why. It's really good. Like a blanket in a bowl.

There's a great debate raging here: skin or no skin. They only stop arguing over this to comment on the weather. Another debate concerns cinnamon sprinkled on top. I voted *yes* but left it out of the recipe in case you belong to the *no* party. Easier to vote on this than the next prime minister election. Talk about the lesser of two evils.

1 cup arborio rice, boiled
3 cups milk
3 eggs, beaten
1 cup sugar
1 tsp vanilla

Directions:

Preheat oven to 325 F / 160 C.

Grease baking dish.

Beat eggs, milk, sugar and vanilla.

Fold in rice.

Bake for 1 hour.

S'mores Cheesecake

My cousin made this for me recently. She wanted to freeze the leftover cake but we convinced her to leave it out so we could have it the next night as well. That showed considerable restraint by my sister and me because we really wanted to take it home and have it for breakfast. *Cheese*cake – must count as a protein.

S'mores are an American thing. For the readers in Blighty, they are graham crackers (digestive like but crisp and crackery) with marshmallows and chocolate wrapped in foil and thrown in the open fire on a camping trip. They're so gooey and sweet and yummy that you want s'more. Get it?

My son tried to make these on a camping trip on the Isle of Wight. The others kept trying to shove it in banana skins. I love campfire-choco-marshmallow-bananas but it's not the same dammit! For a country that's a billion years old, they really don't get tradition.

Crust:
1/2 c. butter, melted
2 1/4 c. graham cracker crumbs
1/3 c. sugar

Filling:
2 (8 oz.) packages cream cheese, softened
1 can sweetened condensed milk
2 tsp. vanilla
3 eggs
1 c. miniature chocolate chips
1 c. miniature marshmallows

Topping:
1 c. miniature marshmallows
1/2 c. chocolate chips
1 Tbs. butter

Directions:
Preheat oven to 325 F / 150 C

Crust:
Combine butter, graham cracker crumbs and sugar.
Press into the bottom of a 10" springform pan.

Filling:
Beat cream cheese, sweetened condensed milk, and vanilla until smooth.
Add eggs and beat until combined.
Stir in chocolate chips and marshmallows.
Pour over crust.

Bake at 325 degrees F for 40 to 45 minutes, until center is almost set.

Topping:

Remove cheesecake from oven and sprinkle marshmallows over top.

Return to the oven and **bake** another 4 to 6 minutes, until the marshmallows are puffed.

Melt chocolate chips and butter together. **Drizzle** over the marshmallows.

Let **cool** to room temperature and then **refrigerate** overnight.

My cheesecake, pictured above, was made with gluten free chocolate digestives, dairy free cream cheese and diary free custard instead of condensed milk. It's not as pretty as yours will be but it's so delicious that I just wanted to have one I could eat. And it was scrumptious.

Challah Bread Pudding

I've mentioned my best friend from law school, Reyne. When we both left the record company, she to run a restaurant in Montauk and me to become a very minor NYC judge, we did Thanksgiving together for years and she made this recipe one year. I changed the bread and alcohol in the recipe (she used old Italian bread and whiskey) but otherwise it's all hers. She was godmother to my youngest because she was the most significant person to me during his pregnancy. When my son was 5, we lived in the middle of nowhere in England and she was in homeopathy school in Toronto. We spoke over the summer and she told me about her fight with breast cancer. Her mother and grandmother were both survivors and in remission for years. Sometime later, her boyfriend told me she died. Turns out she died on her godson's birthday.

I keep a picture of us from my wedding by the kettle and say hello to her every morning to make amends for the stretches where we didn't speak often enough. You know what? Take 5 minutes before you start cooking and call an old friend.

1 loaf of old bread, Challah if you have
1 large pot of custard
¼ cup of Frangelico or amaretto liqueur
1 cup of dark chocolate chips
½ tsp salt
Butter for greasing
Strawberries for garnish

Directions:

Grease baking dish with butter.

Mix liqueur with custard.

Add bread.

Sprinkle salt and chocolate chips on top.

Cover with cling film and **weight** with a plate.

Preheat oven to 350 F for 20 minutes.

Remove plate and cling film.

Bake pudding for 15 minutes.

Add strawberries just before eating. The sharpness cuts the richness beautifully.

Reyne and me on my wedding day. The photo is stuck to the glass and when I tried to remove it, it started to tear and peel. So it sits with its broken glass and unprotected surface in my kitchen still. I treasure it.

A Gefilte Fish Out Of Water by Stacey Haber

Thank You

One of my favorite prayers is the Sh'ma, which I recited with my children before sleeping and upon waking. Also upon embarking on a long trip. I also think it's the best way of thanking G-d, by proclaiming his omnipotence and sovereignty.

I have my children say the English as well every now and then so the words don't lose their meaning.

I think it's also the best way to end this book. Thank you.

Engllish
Hear, O Israel: the Lord our G-d, the Lord is One.

(whispered) Blessed is the Name of His glorious kingdom for all eternity.

You shall love the Lord your G-d with all your heart, with all your soul and with all your might. And these words which I command you this day shall be on your heart. You shall teach them to your children, and you shall speak of them when you sit in your house and when you walk on the way, when you lie down and when you rise up. You shall bind them as a sign upon your arm, and they shall be for a reminder between your eyes. And you shall write them upon the doorposts of your house and upon your gates.

Phonetic
Sh'ma Yis-ra-eil, A-do-nai E-lo-hei-nu, A-do-nai E-chad.

(whispered) Ba-ruch sheim k'vod mal-chu-to l'o-lam va-ed.

V'a-hav-ta eit A-do-nai E-lo-he-cha, B'chawl l'va-v'cha, u-v'chawl naf-sh'cha, u-v'chawl m'o-de-cha. V'ha-yu ha-d'va-rim ha-ei-leh, A-sher a-no-chi m'tsa-v'cha ha-yom, al l'va-ve-cha. V'shi-nan-tam l'-va-ne-cha, v'di-bar-ta bam, b'shiv-t'cha b'vei-te-cha, uv-lech-t'cha va-de-rech,u-v'shawch-b'cha uv-ku-me-cha. Uk-shar-tam l'ot al ya-de-cha, v'ha-yu l'to-ta-fot bein ei-ne-cha. Uch-tav-tam, al m'zu-zot bei-te-cha, u-vish-a-re-cha.

Hebrew

שְׁמַע יִשְׂרָאֵל יְיָ אֱלֹהֵינוּ יְיָ אֶחָד

בָּרוּךְ שֵׁם כְּבוֹד מַלְכוּתוֹ לְעוֹלָם וָעֶד

וְאָהַבְתָּ אֵת יְיָ אֱלֹהֶיךָ בְּכָל לְבָבְךָ וּבְכָל נַפְשְׁךָ וּבְכָל מְאֹדֶךָ
וְהָיוּ הַדְּבָרִים הָאֵלֶּה אֲשֶׁר אָנֹכִי מְצַוְּךָ הַיּוֹם עַל לְבָבֶךָ
וְשִׁנַּנְתָּם לְבָנֶיךָ וְדִבַּרְתָּ בָּם
בְּשִׁבְתְּךָ בְּבֵיתֶךָ וּבְלֶכְתְּךָ בַדֶּרֶךְ וּבְשָׁכְבְּךָ וּבְקוּמֶךָ
וּקְשַׁרְתָּם לְאוֹת עַל יָדֶךָ וְהָיוּ לְטֹטָפֹת בֵּין עֵינֶיךָ
וּכְתַבְתָּם עַל מְזֻזוֹת בֵּיתֶךָ וּבִשְׁעָרֶיךָ

About the Author

Stacey is the author of screenplays, TV shows, cookbooks, novels, stage plays, children's stories and books about the business of music.

Originally from New York City, the tug of historic heart strings, great architecture and lovely people pulled her to London in 1981 and she hasn't been able to stay away for very long. She is a member of the National Union of Journalists and The Society of Authors.

All the pottery and paintings are by Stacey. All photos are by Stacey unless otherwise noted.
The pottery was made at Milland Pottery under the tutelage of Angela Carter.
@LoveStaceyPottery

Photo by Lorraine Lucas
Blossom & Bone Photography

A Gefilte Fish Out Of Water by Stacey Haber

A Gefilte Fish Out Of Water by Stacey Haber

A Gefilte Fish Out Of Water by Stacey Haber

Recipe Index

BV - #0024 - 070121 - C95 - 297/210/7 - PB - 9781916036390 - Gloss Lamination